Waterfowl
Coloring Book

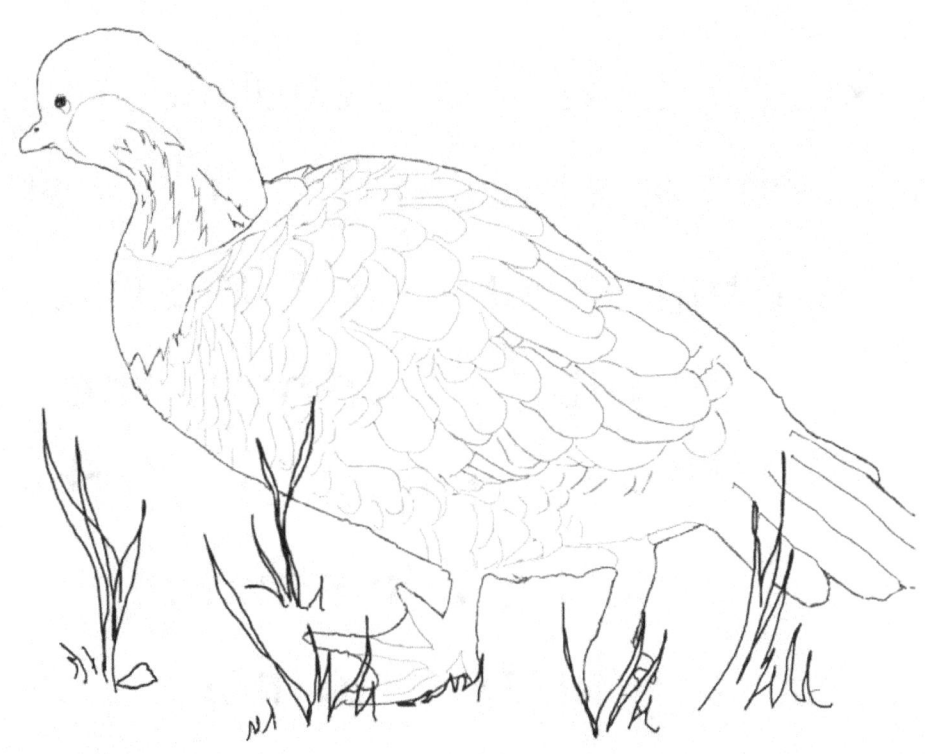

Illustrations by
Kitty Fournier

Waterfowl Coloring Book

Dedicated to my wonderful family who always encourage me in my artistic endeavors.

Other books by Kitty Fournier

Parrot Coloring Book

Butterfly & Moth Coloring Book

Stained Glass Animals Coloring Book

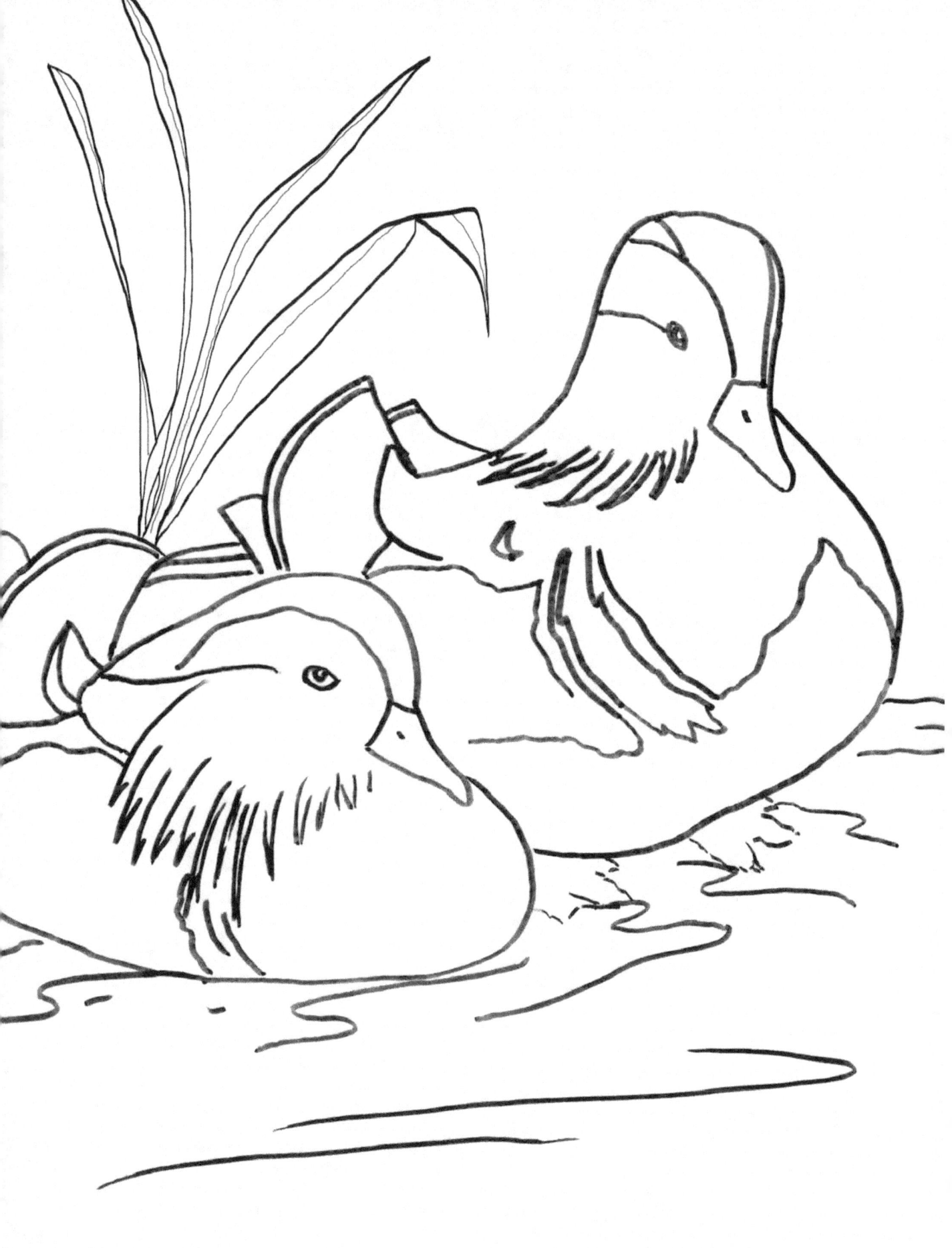

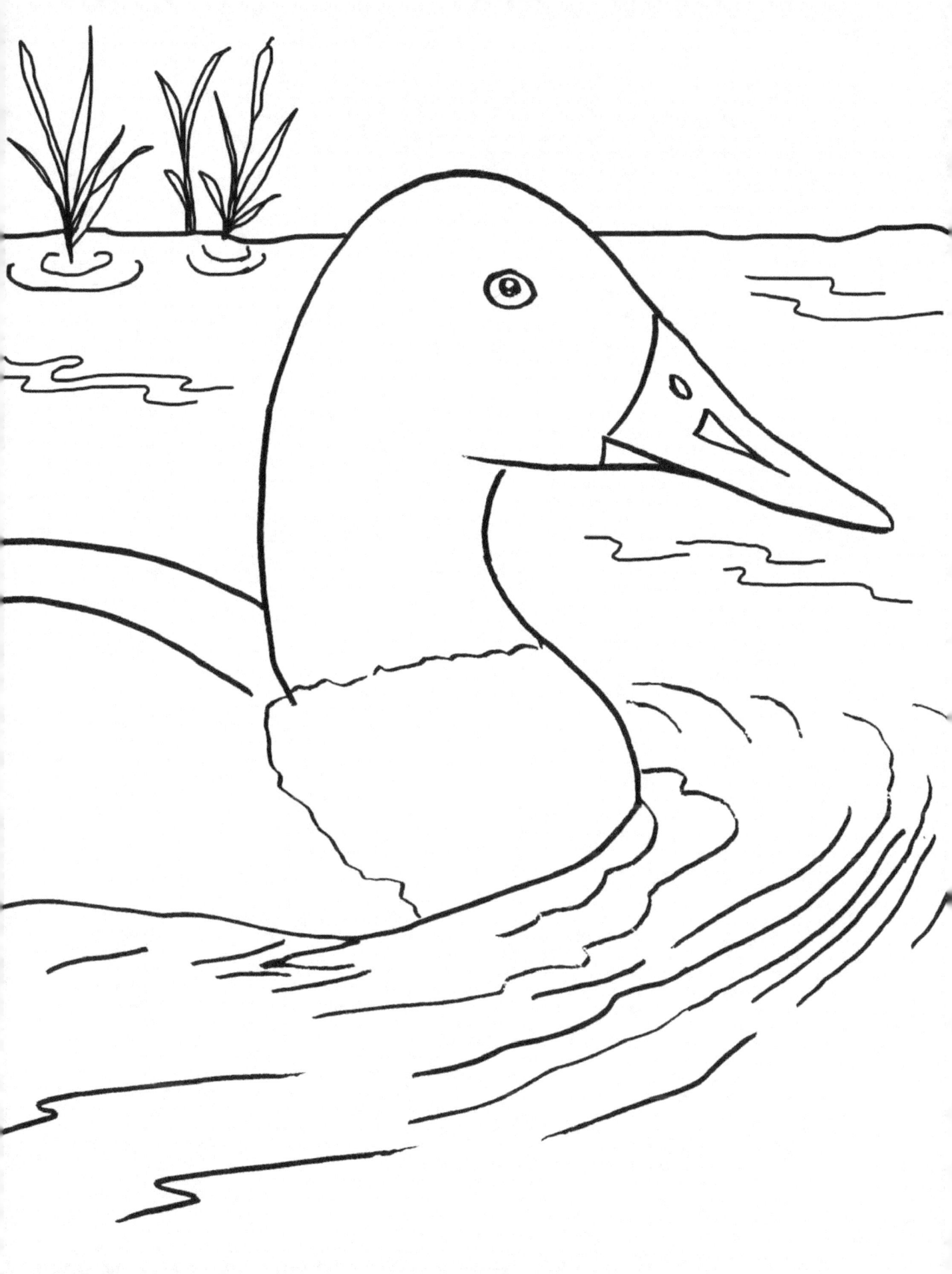

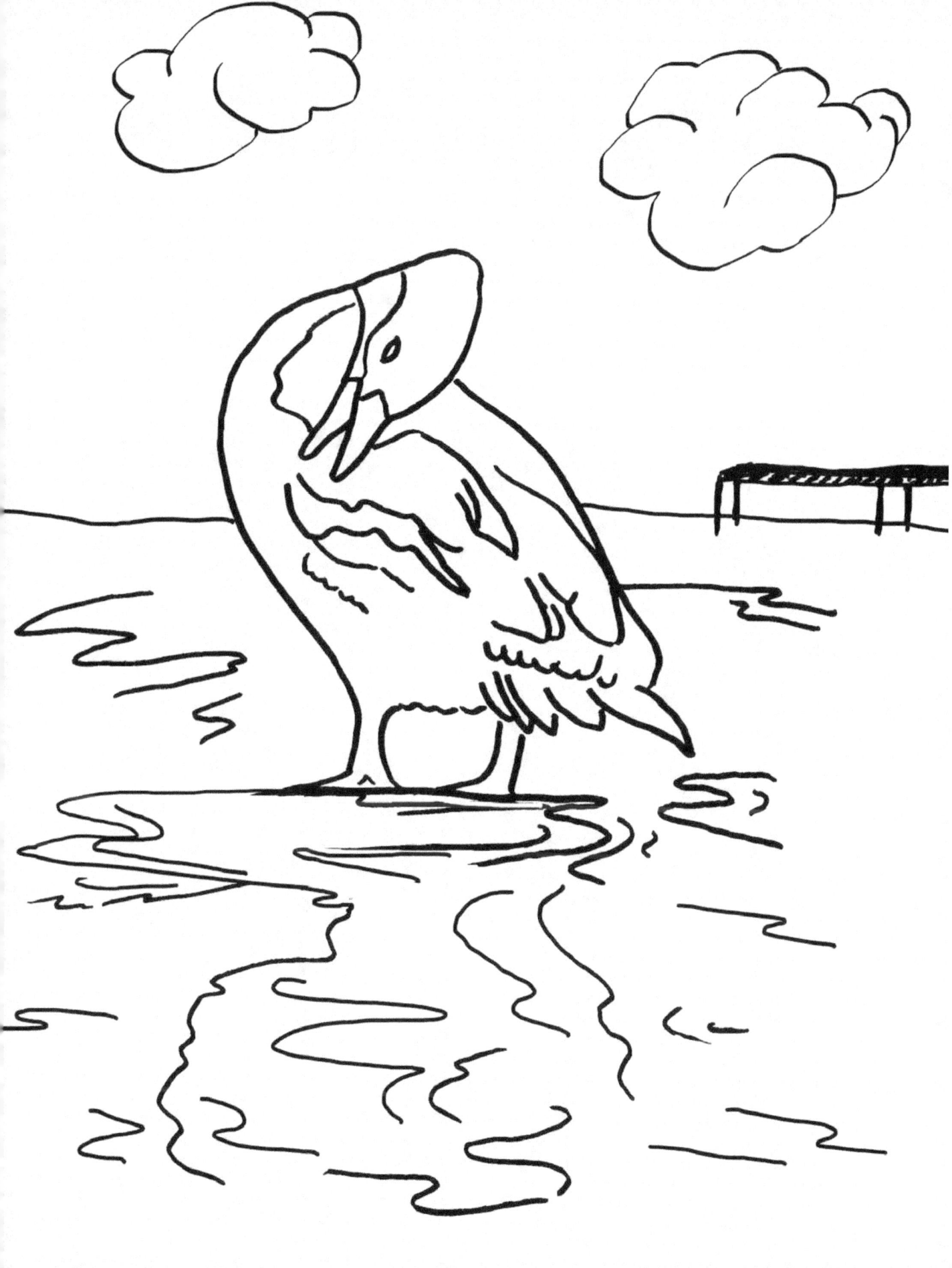

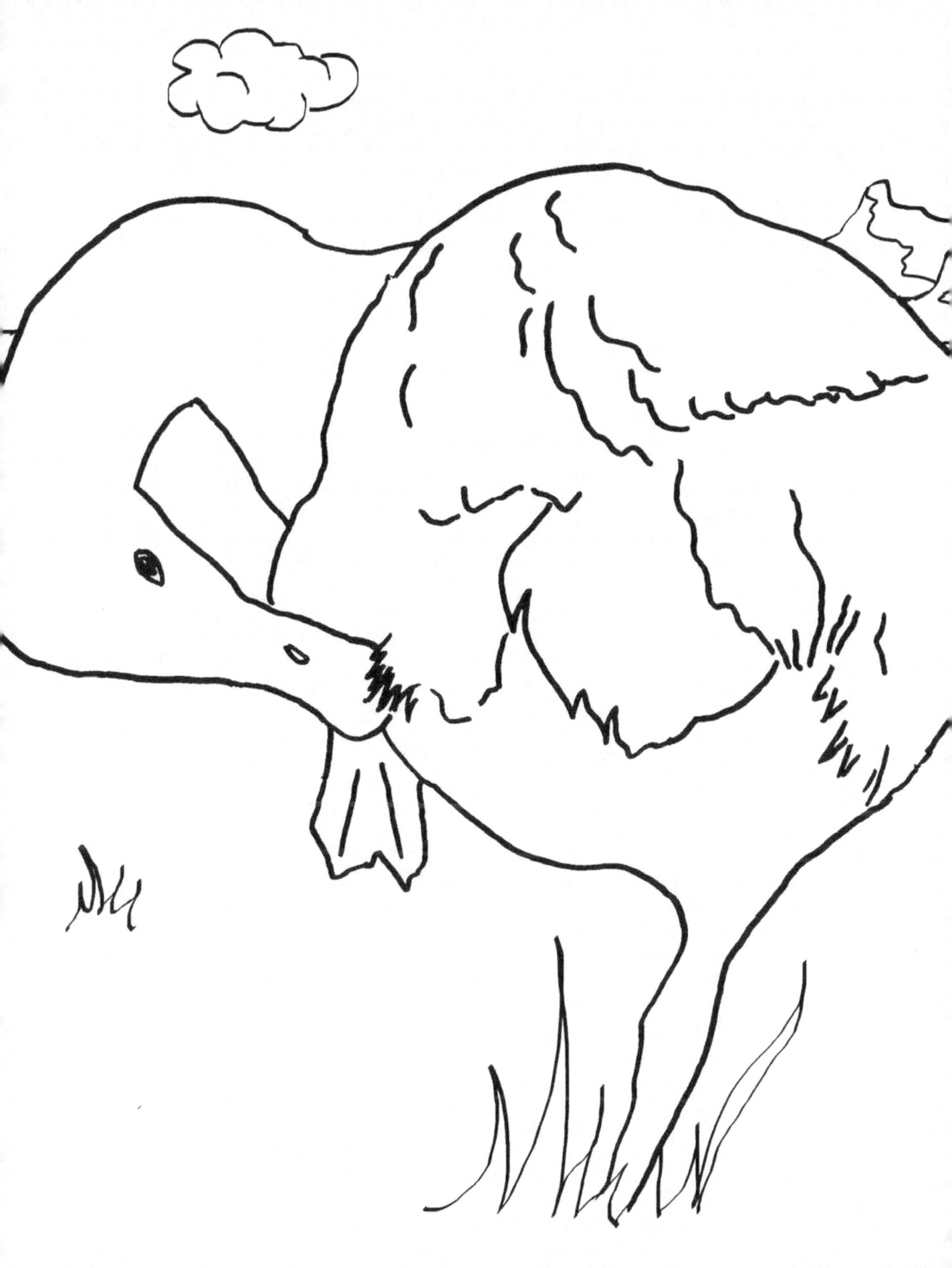

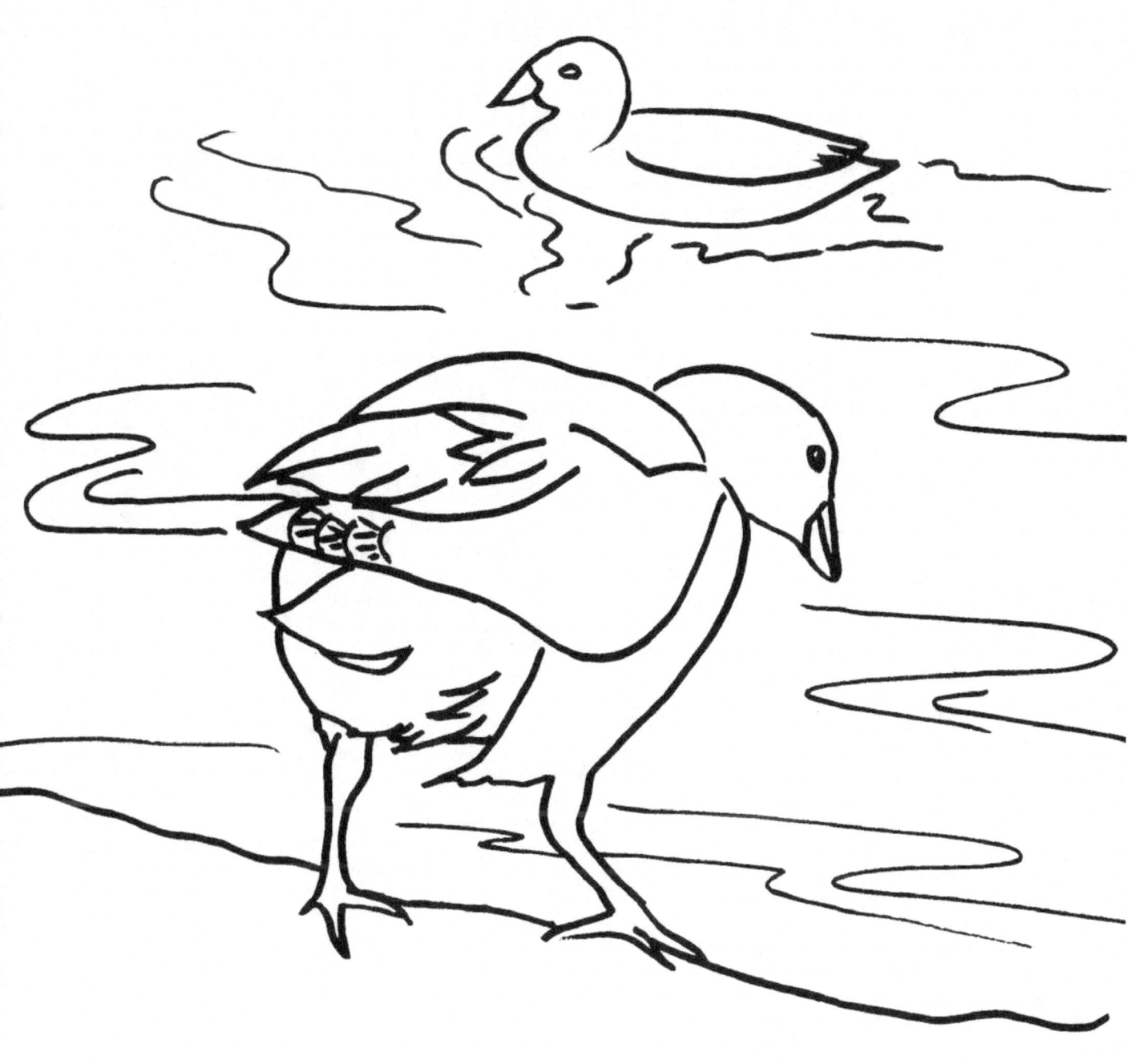

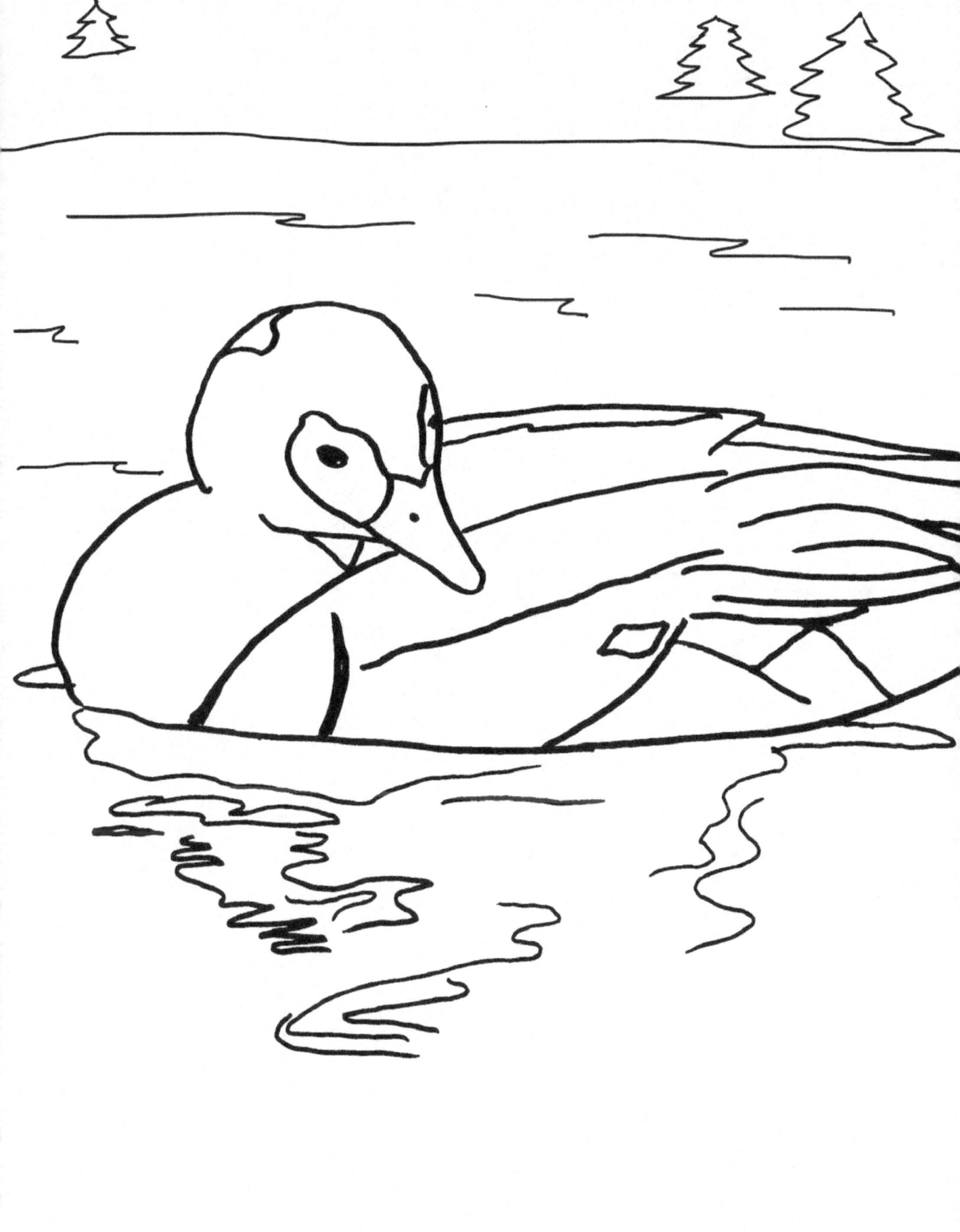

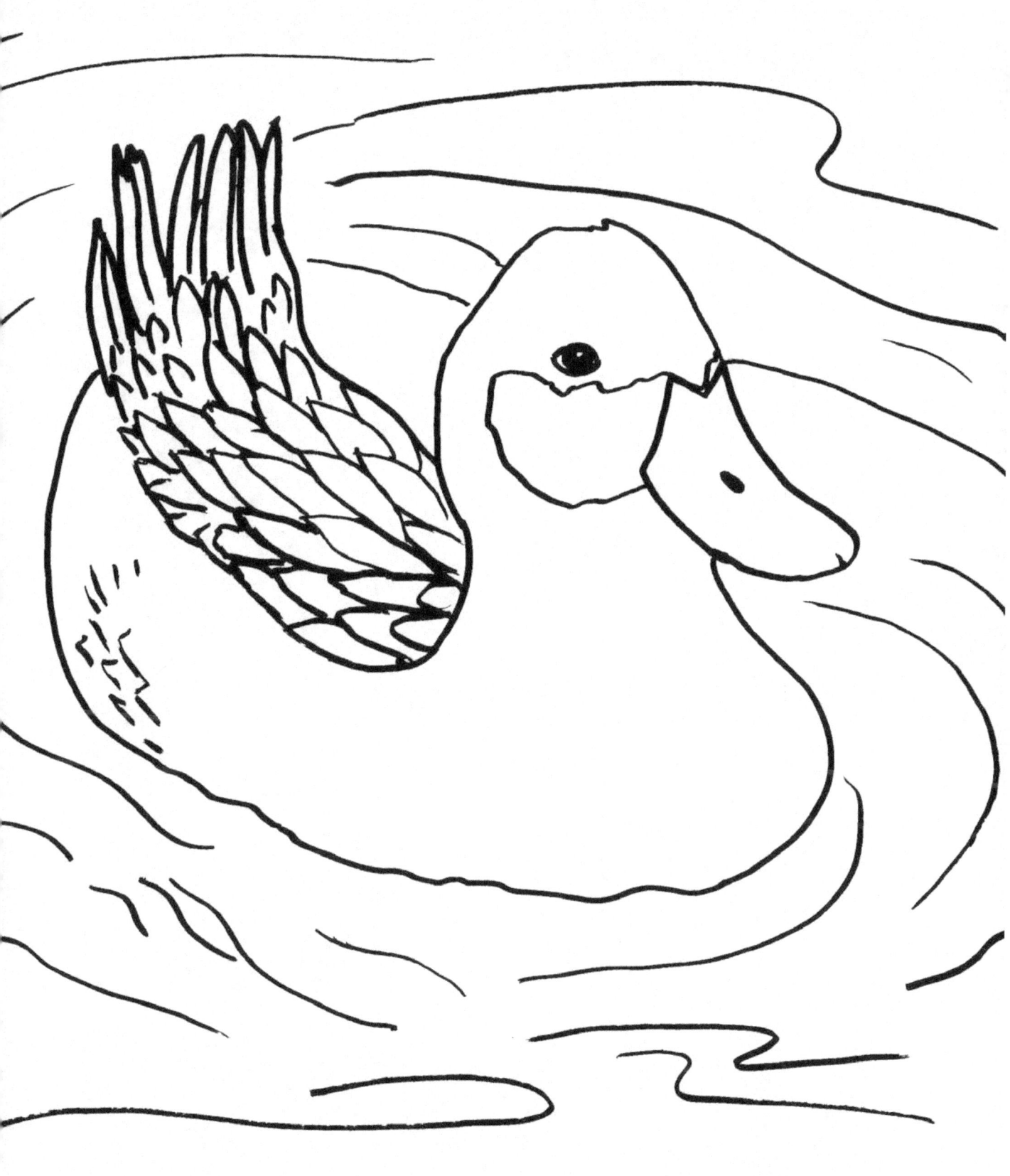

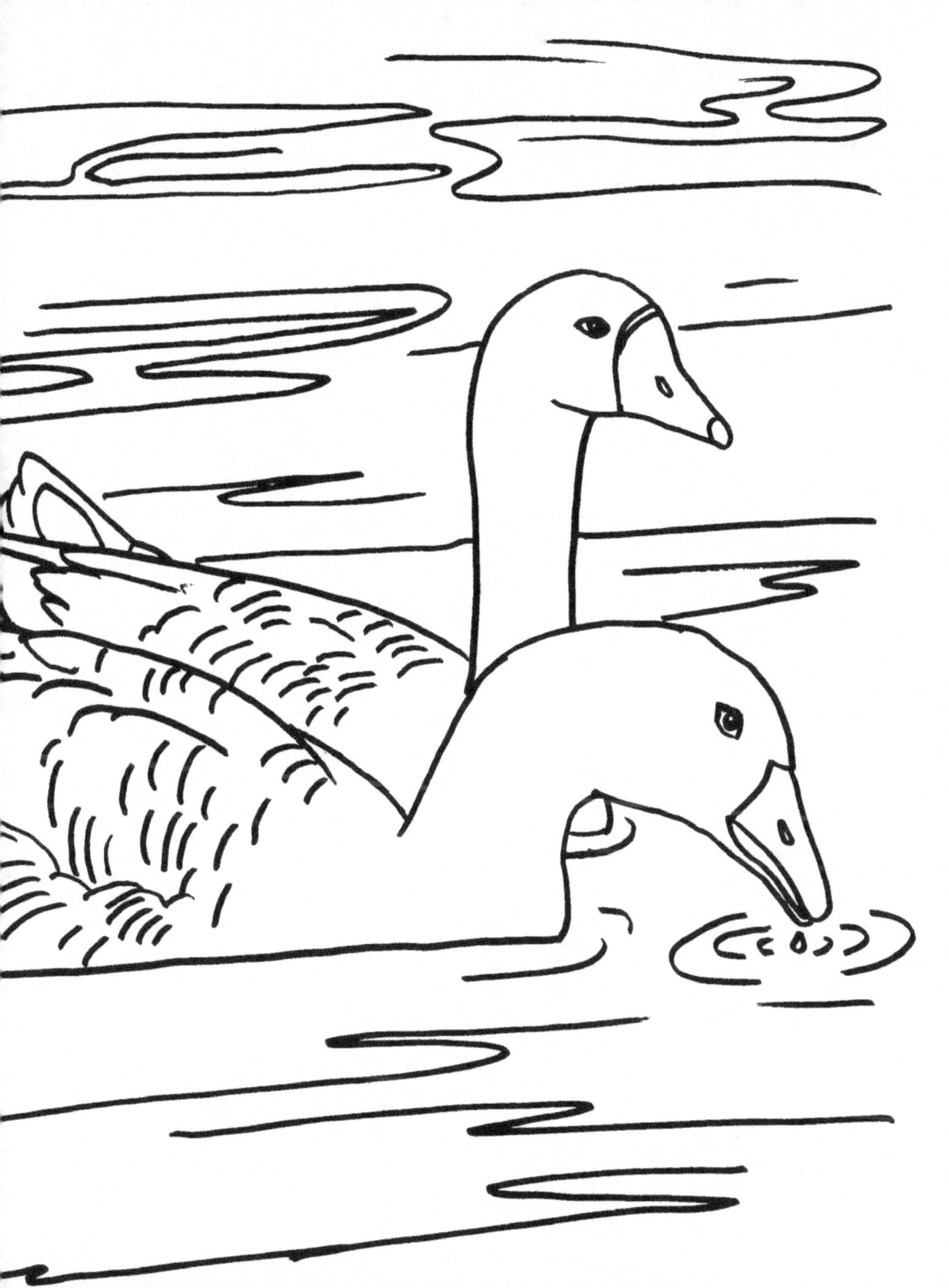

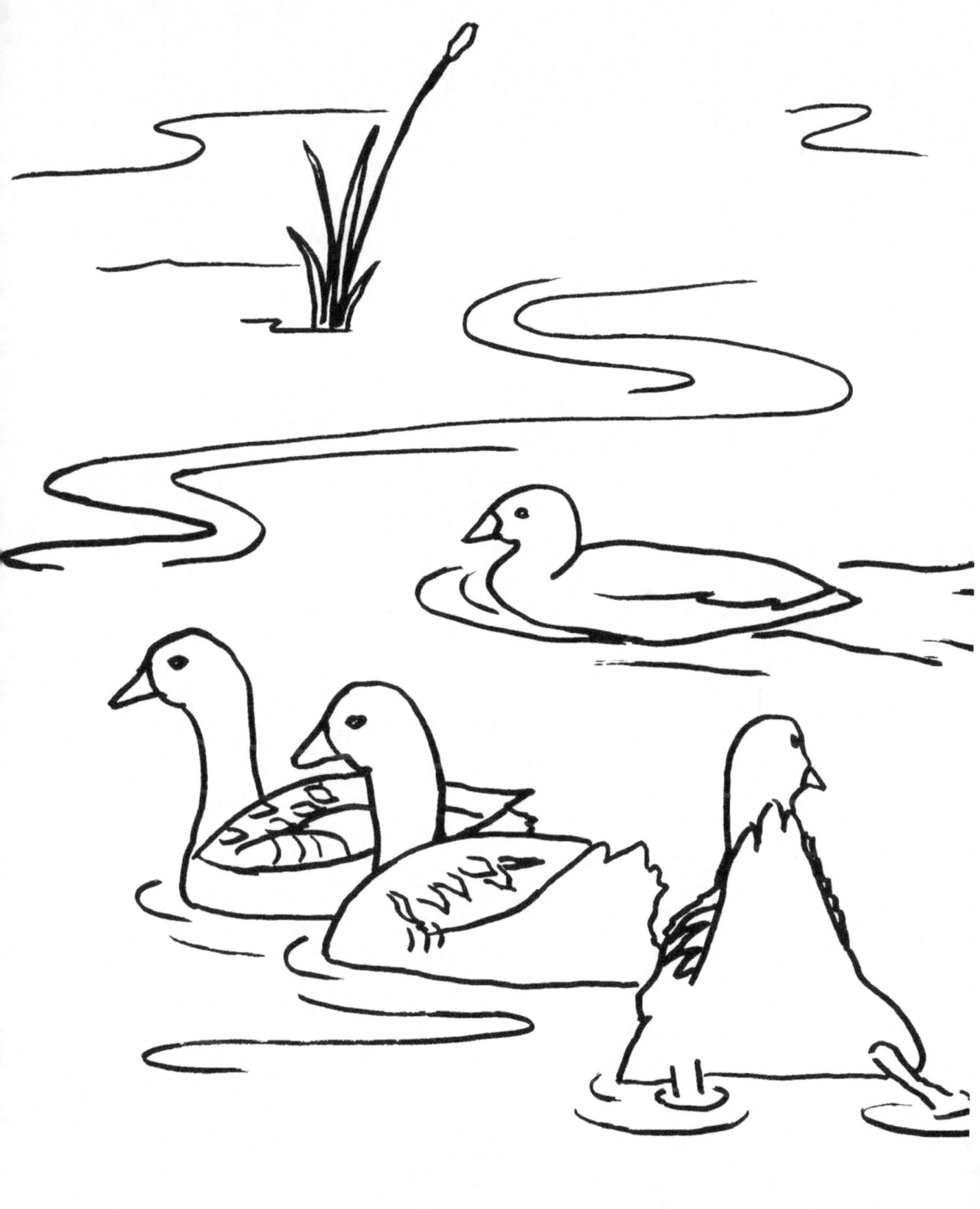

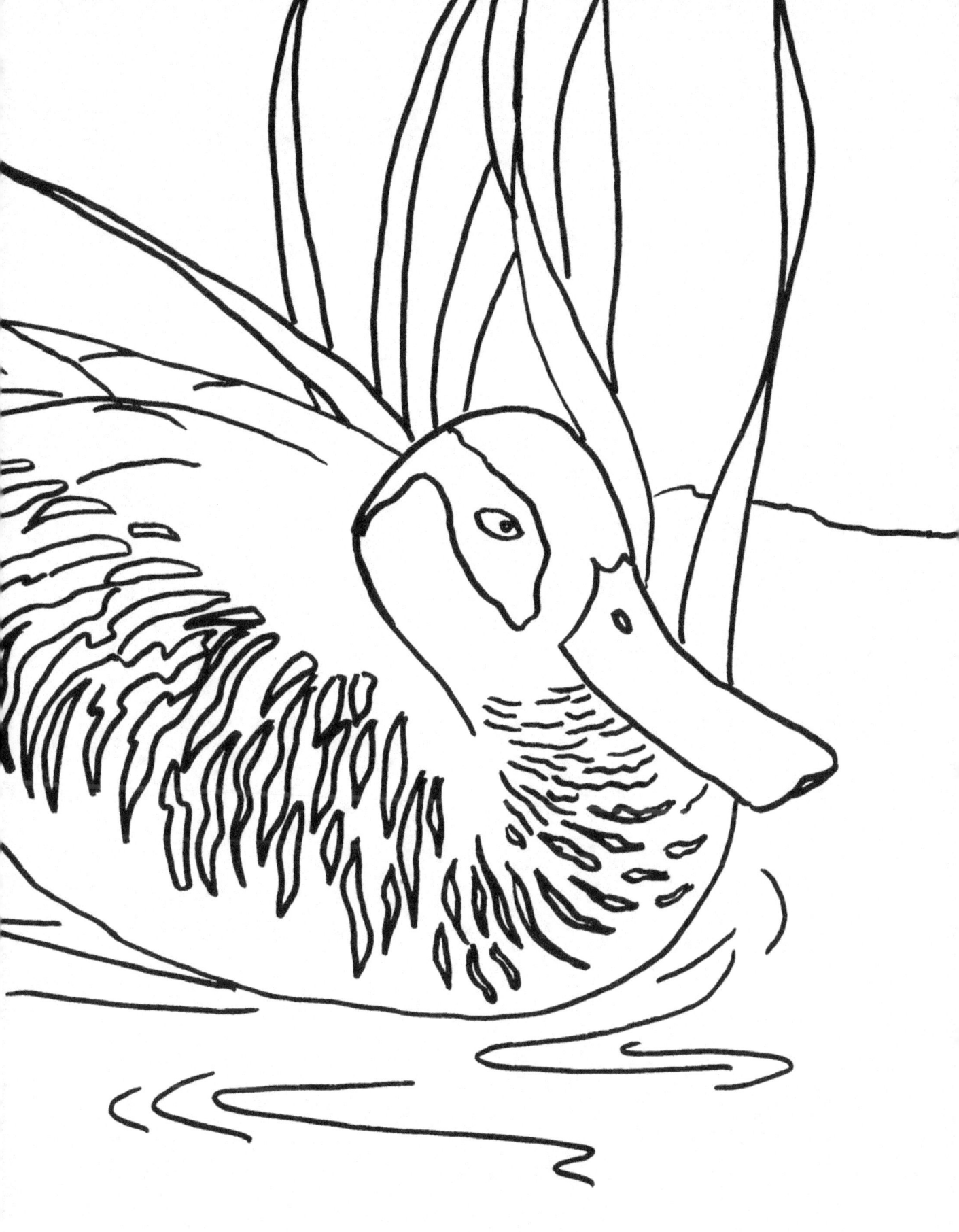

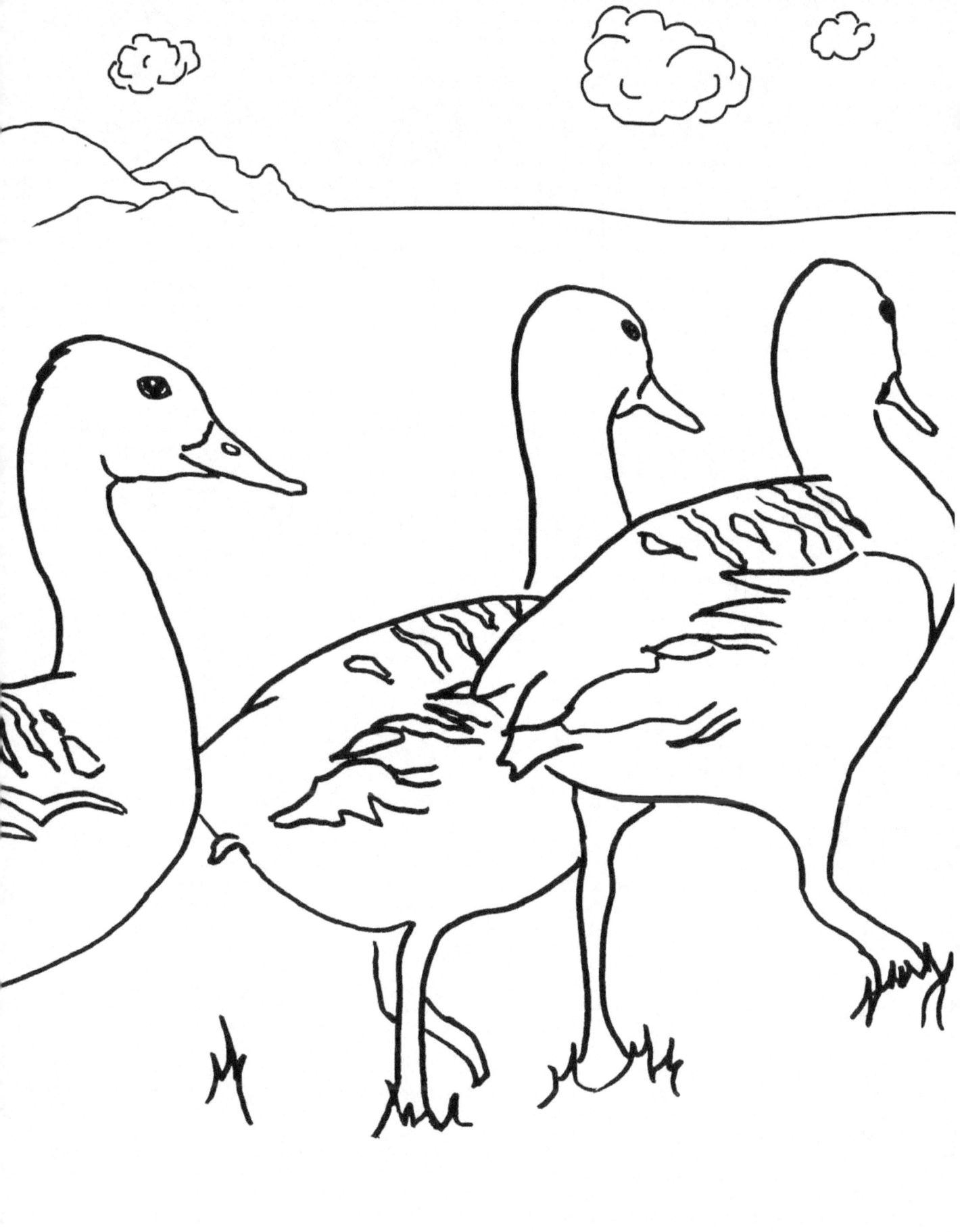

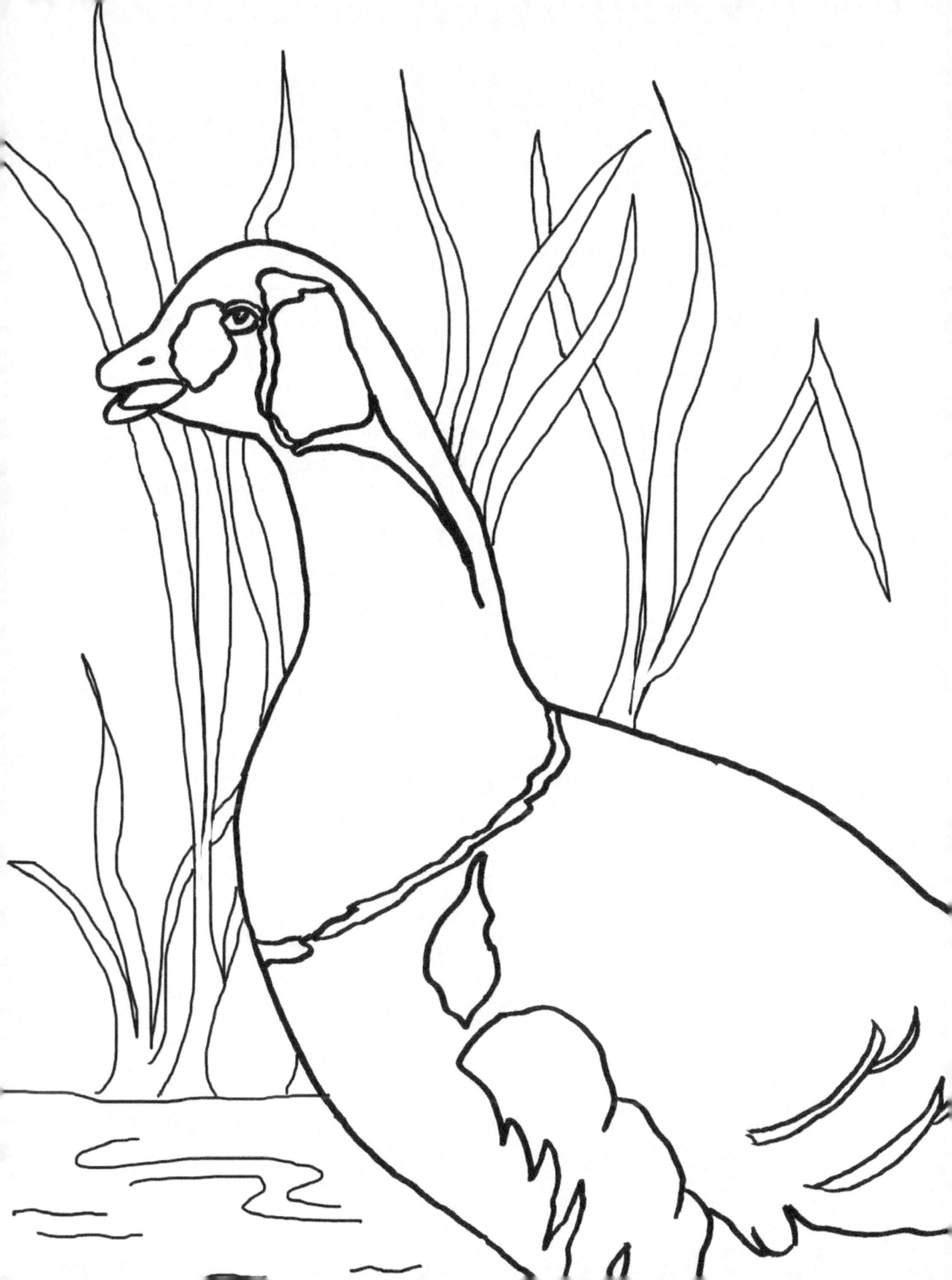

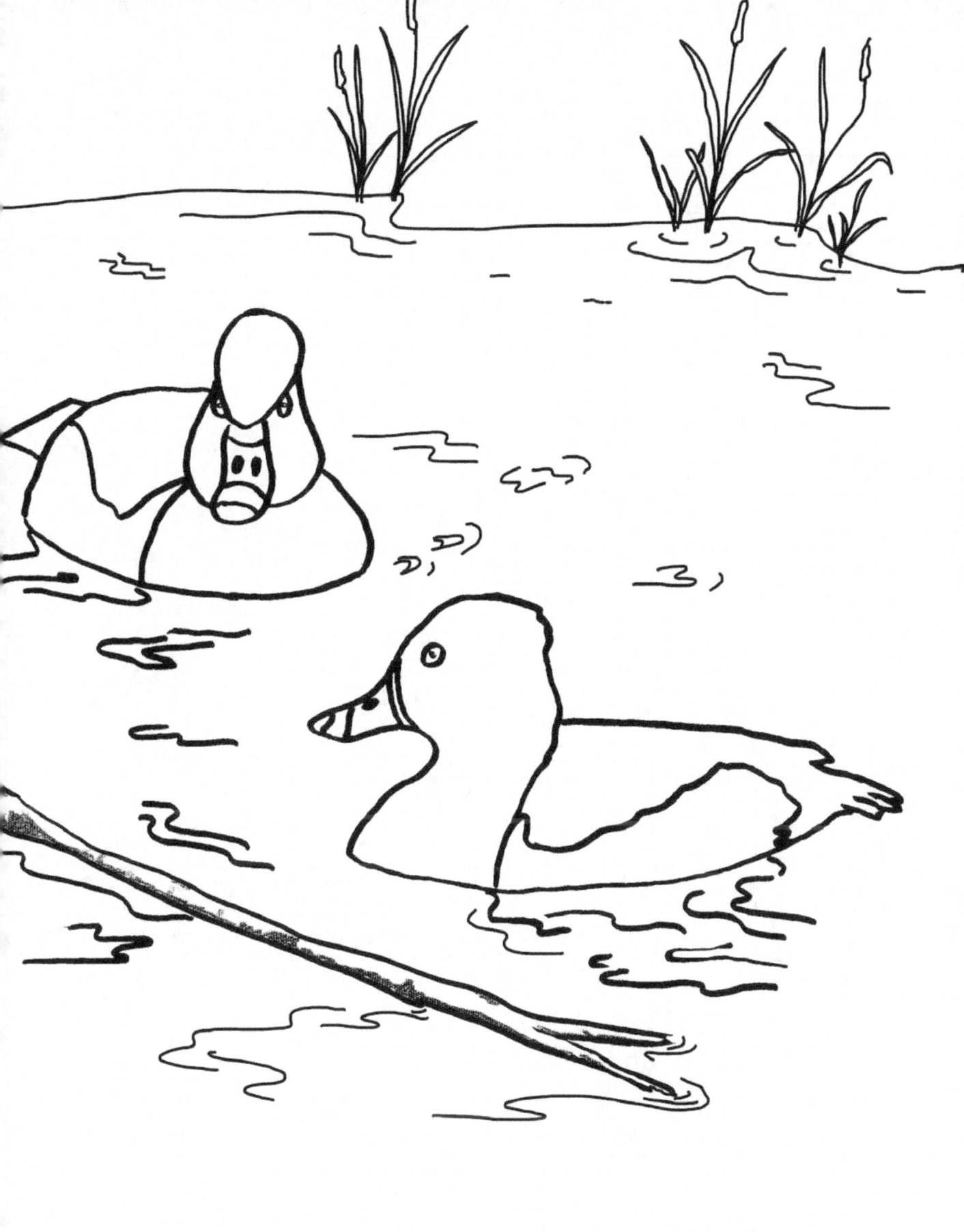

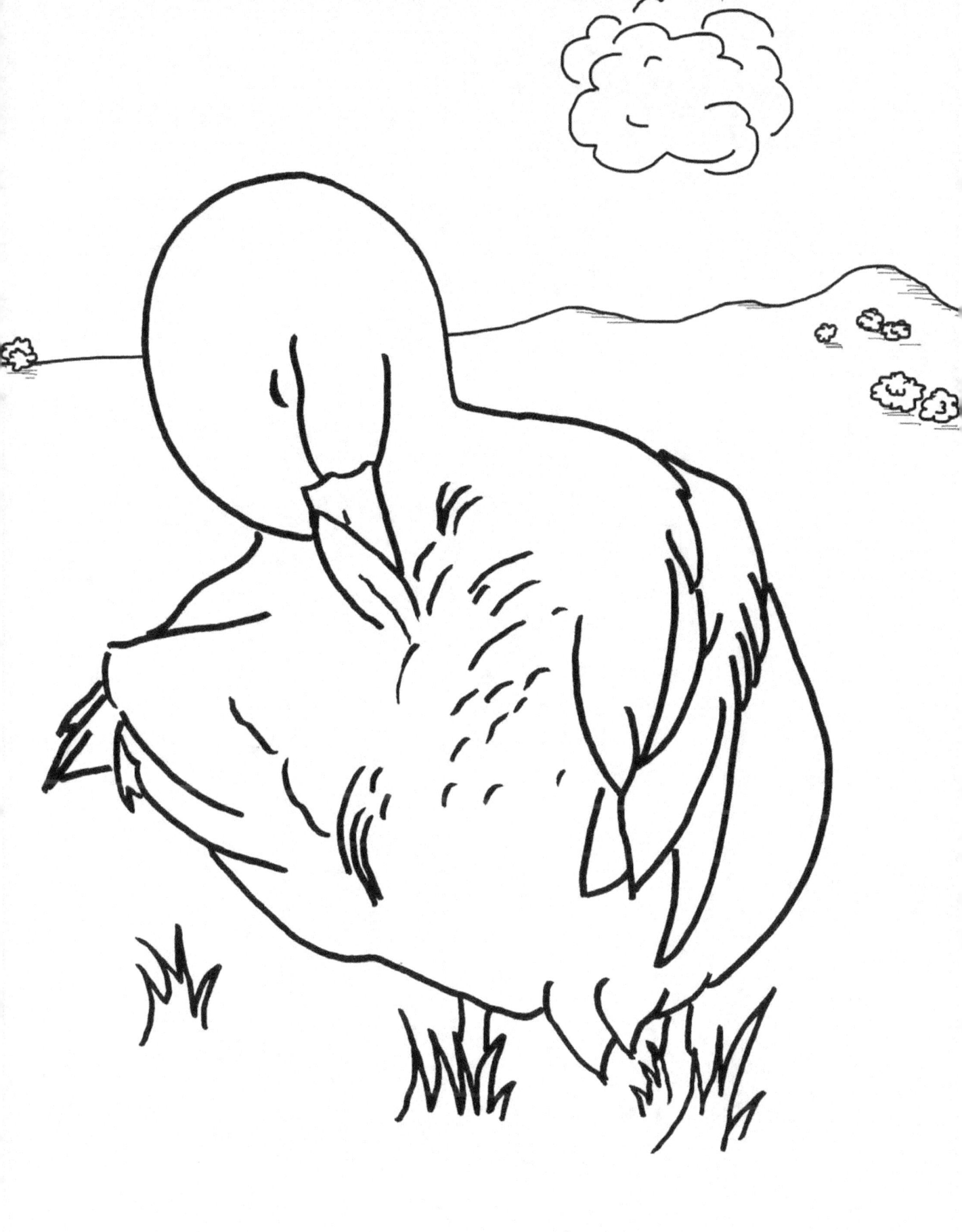

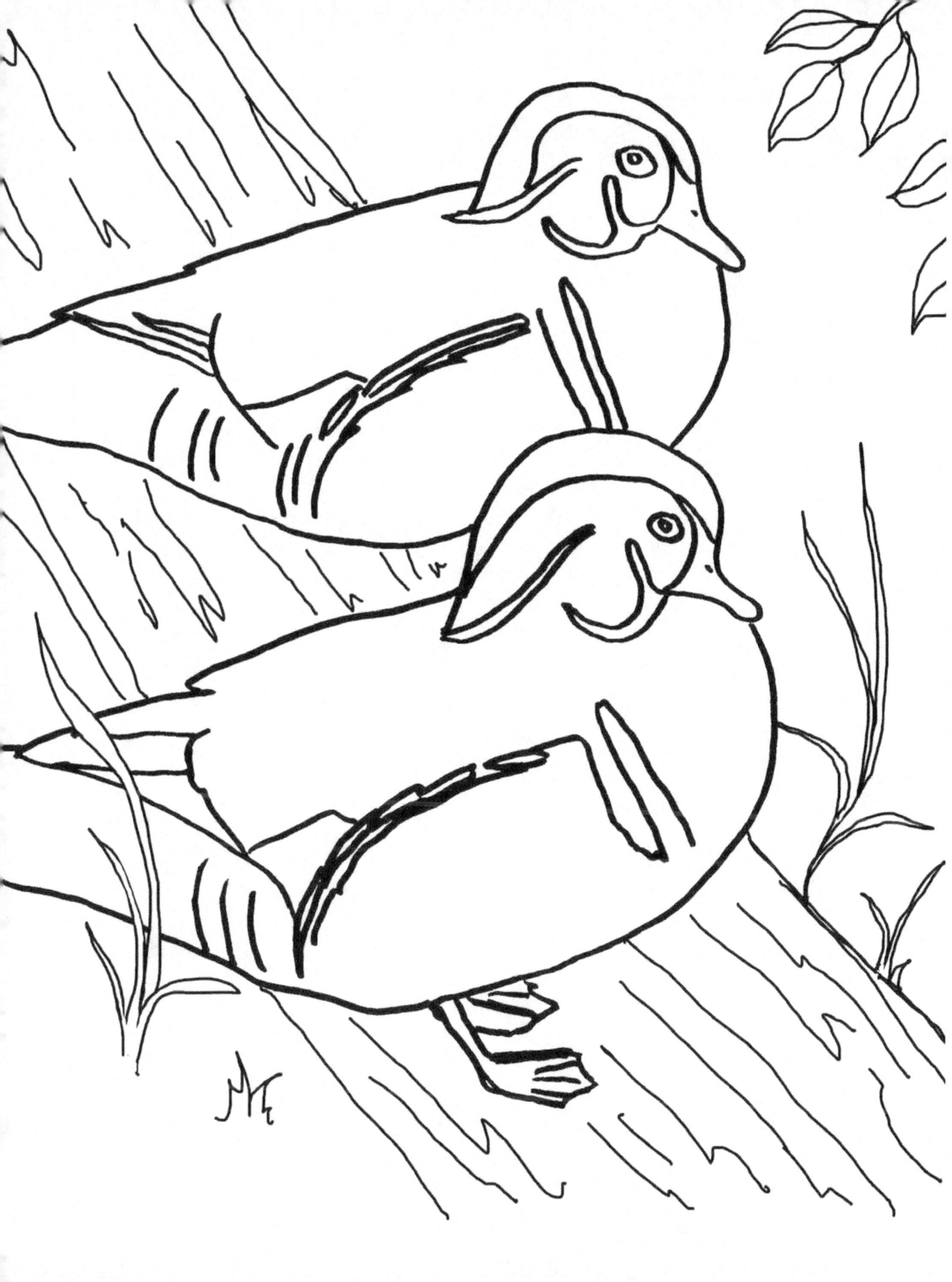

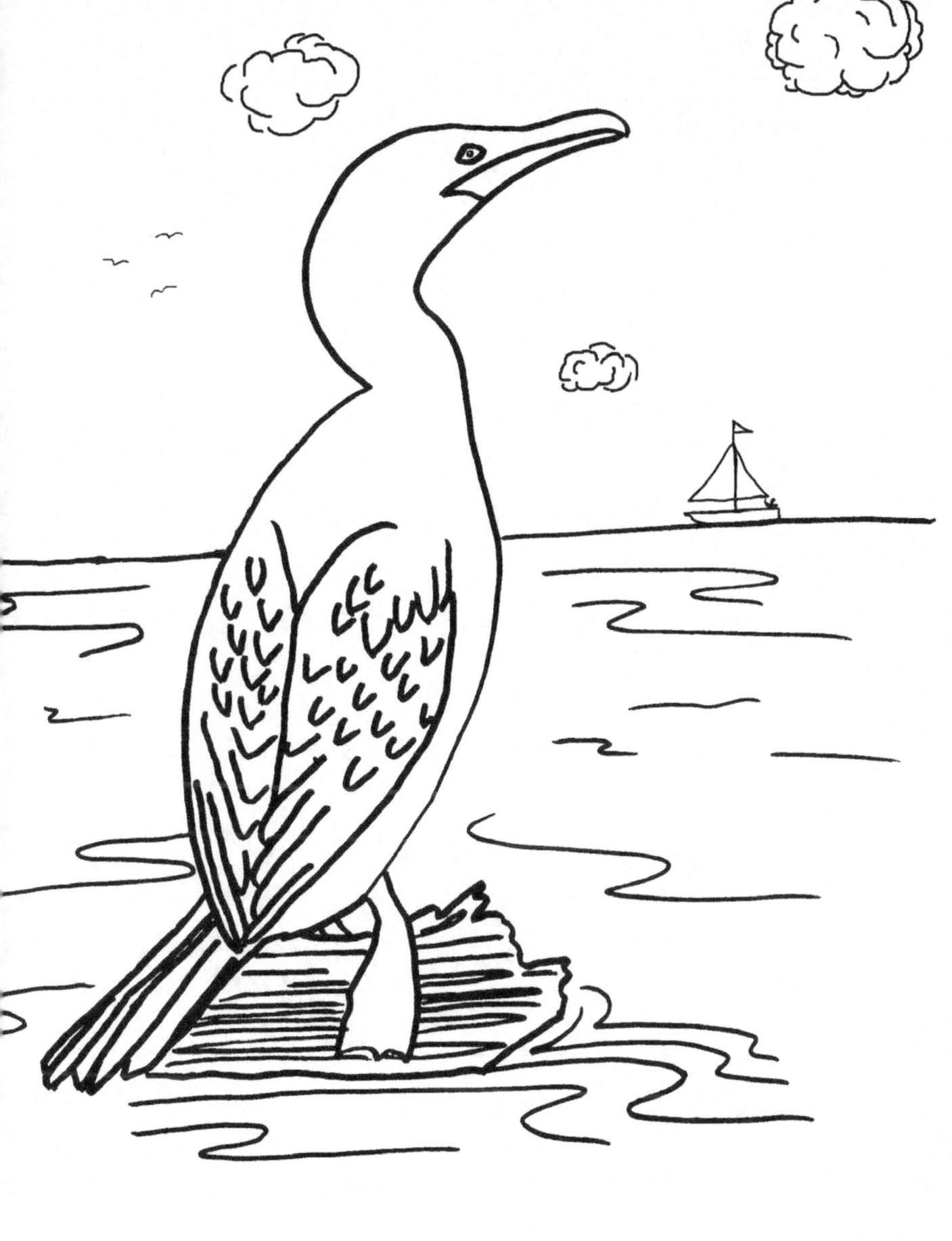

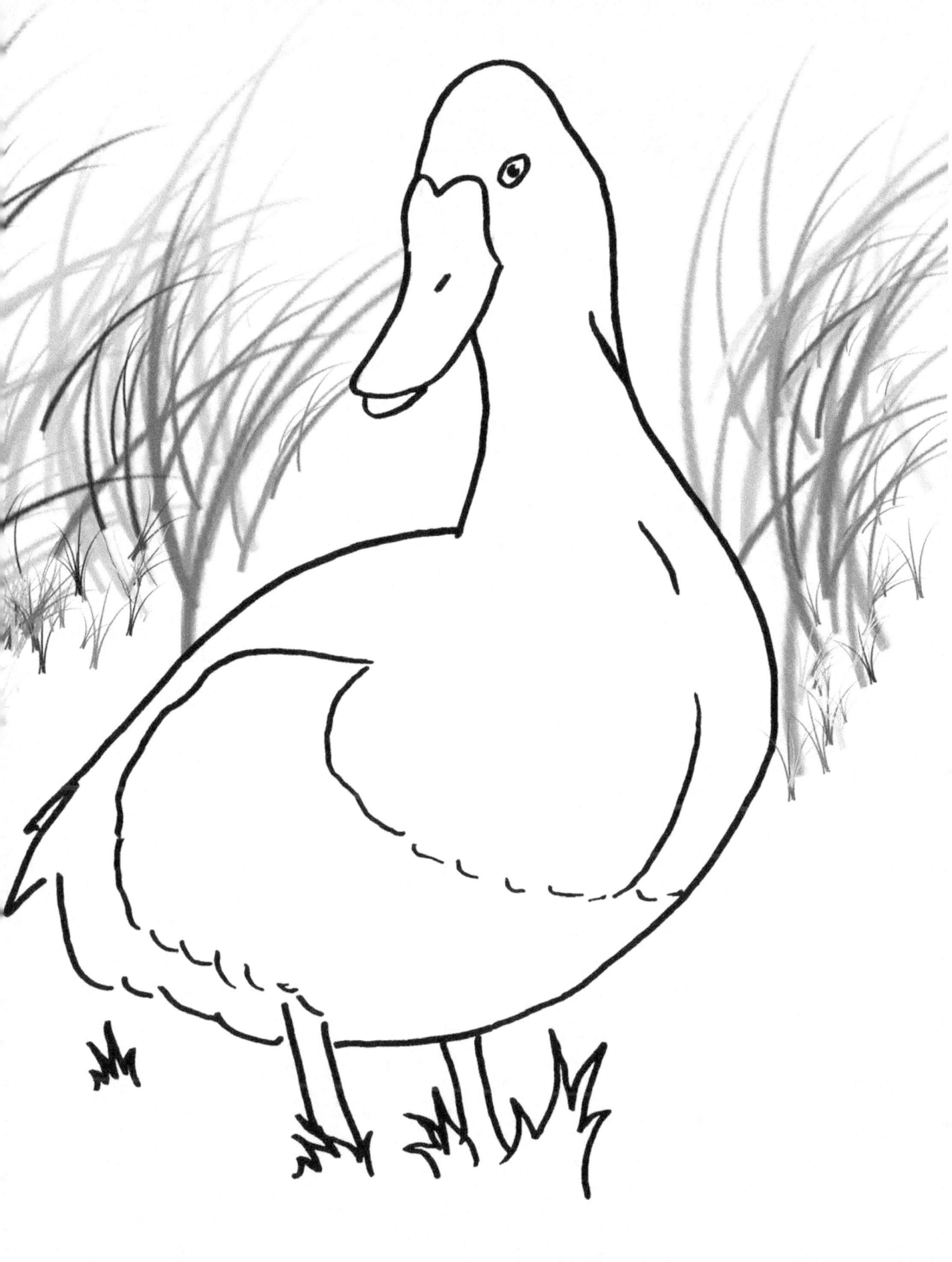

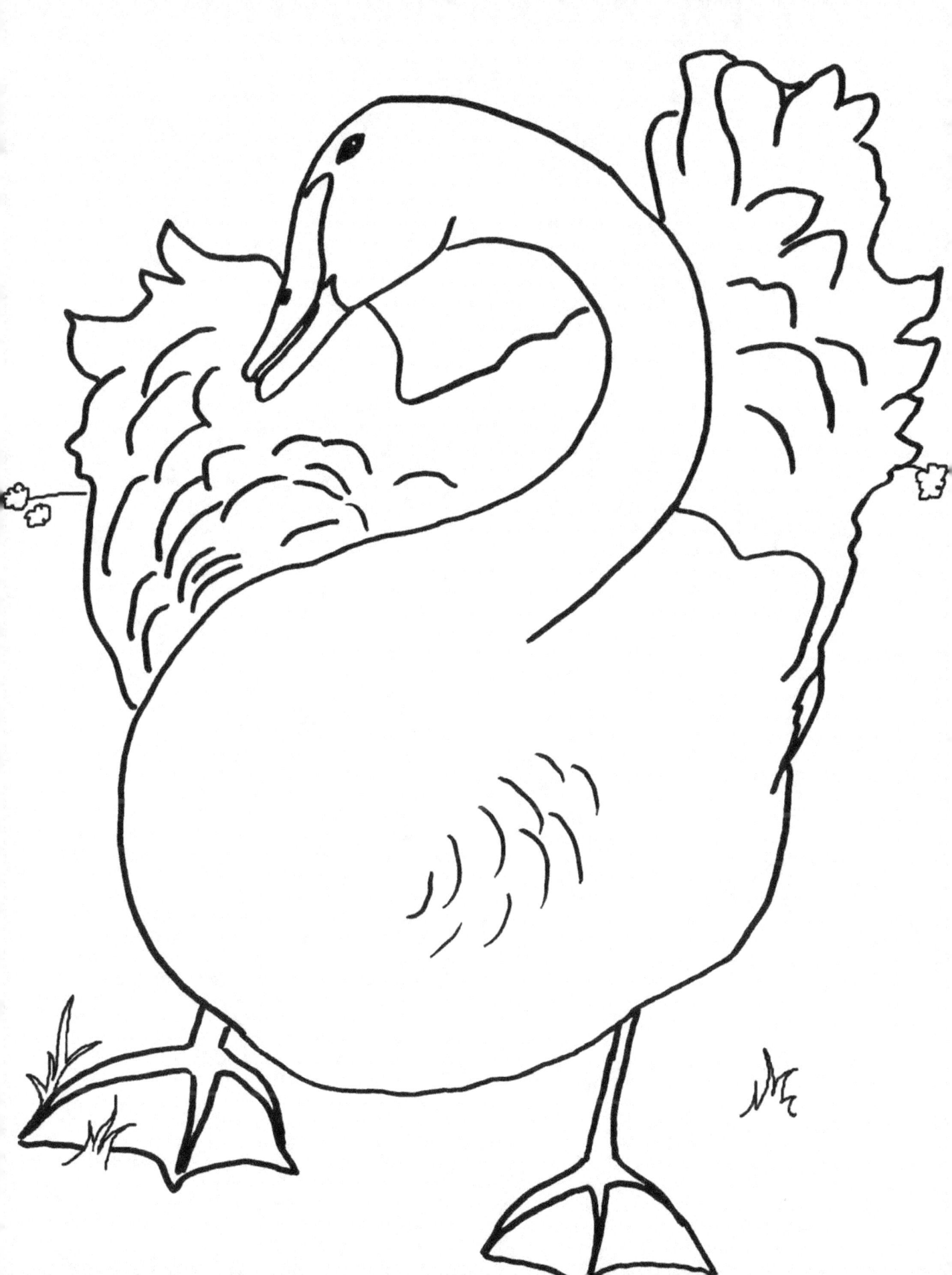

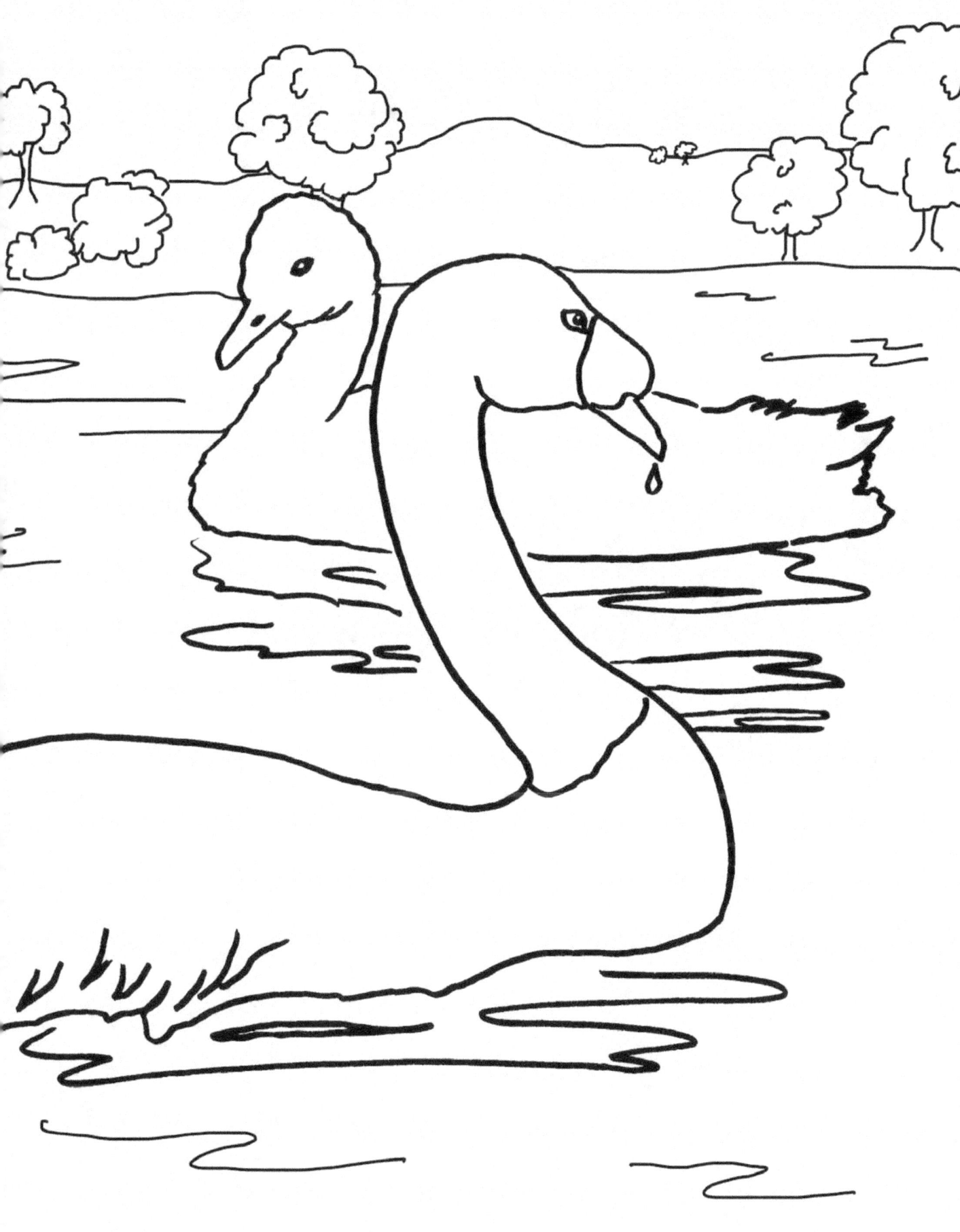

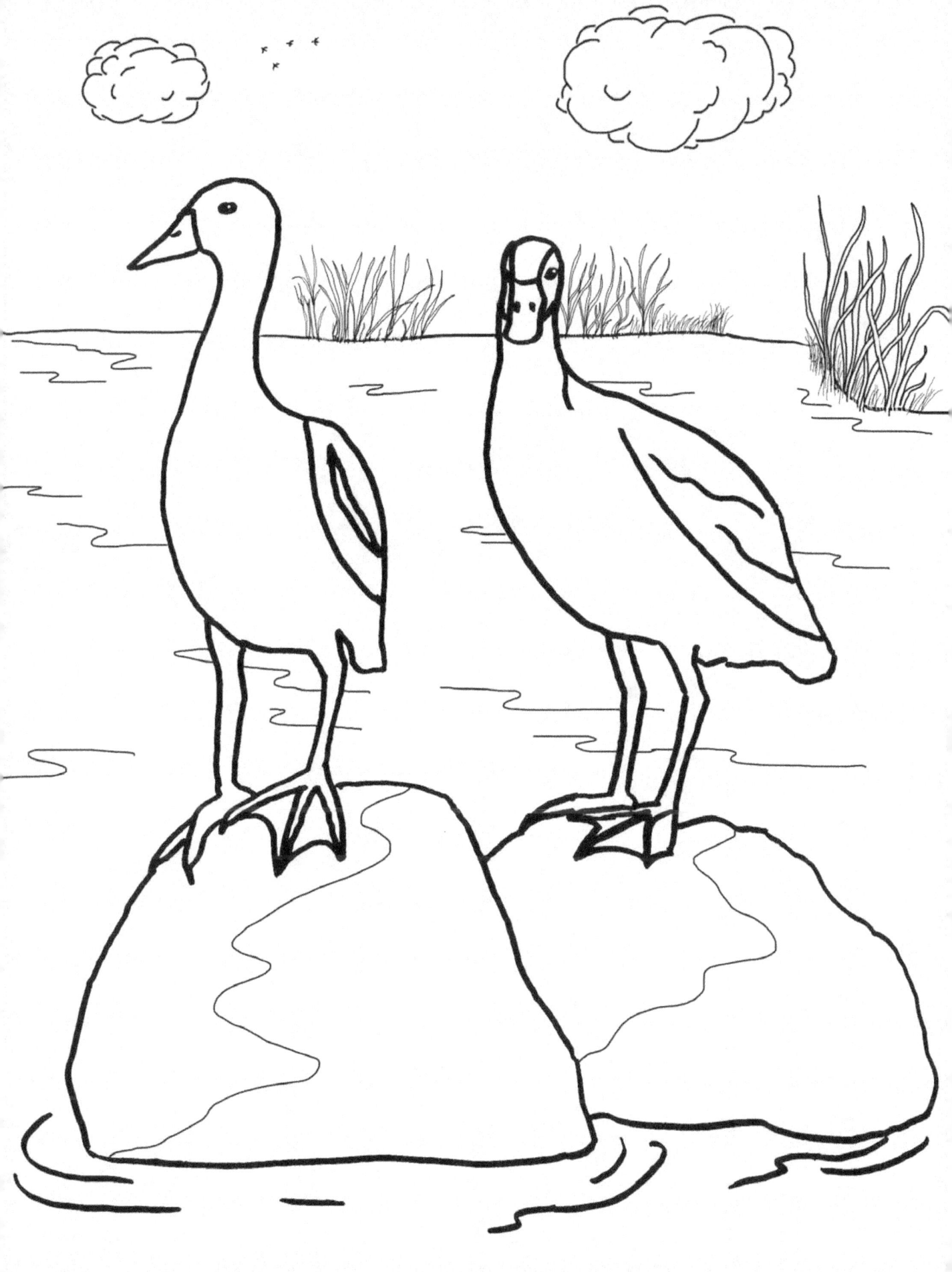

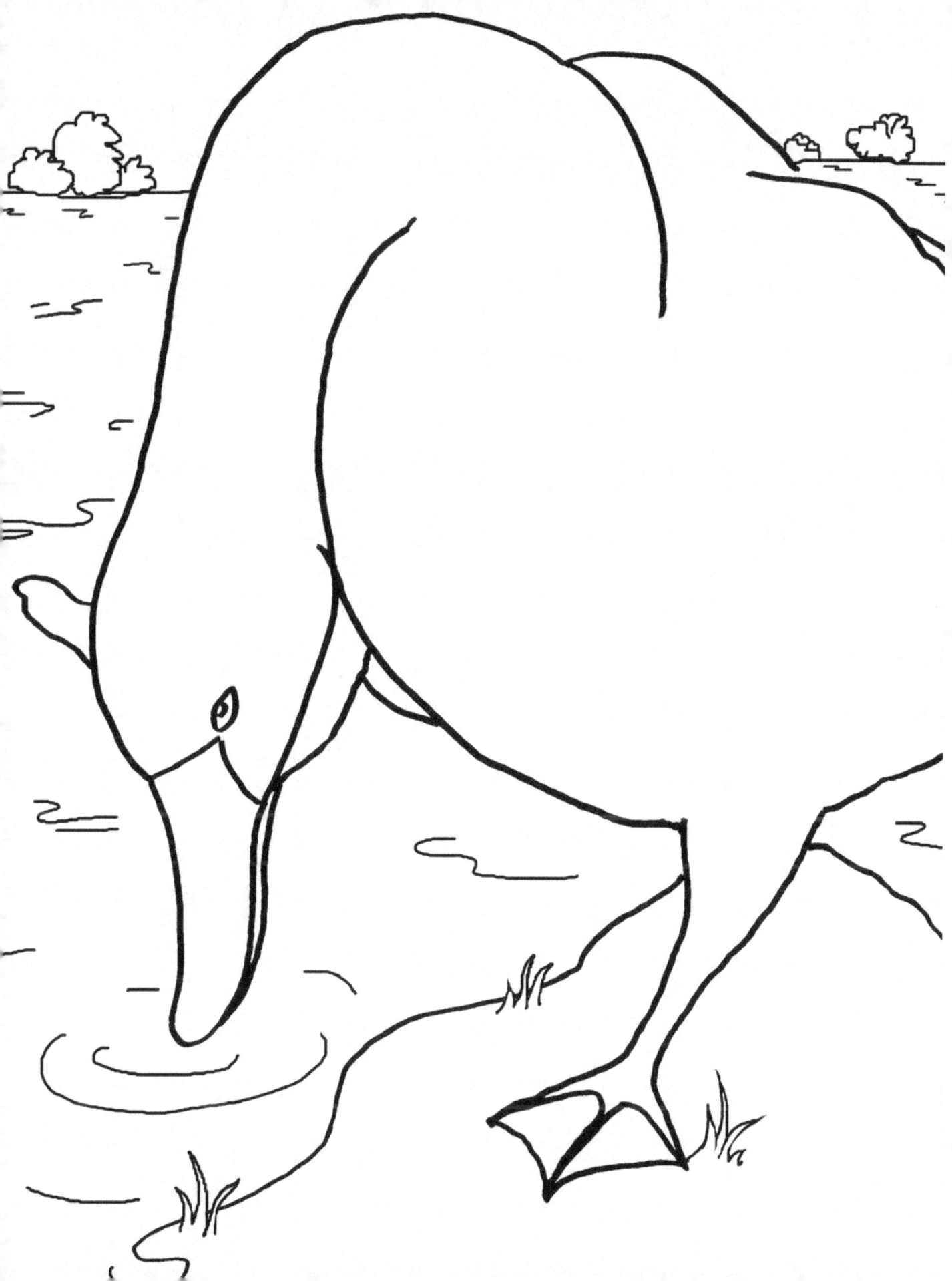

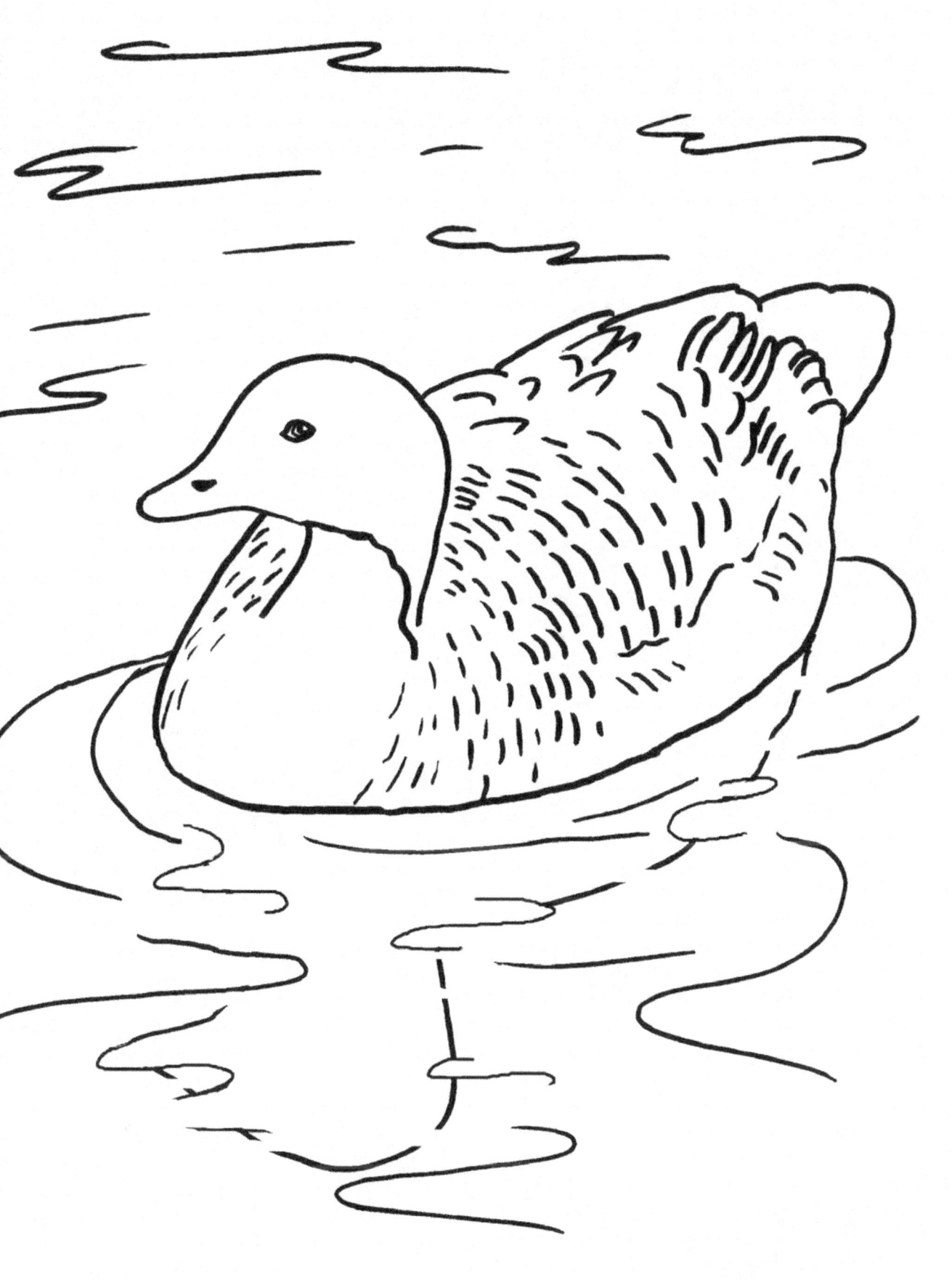